Time to Celebrate!

LET'S GO TO A BIRTHDAY PARTY!

By Benjamin Proudfit

Gareth Stevens
PUBLISHING

Please visit our website, www.garethstevens.com. For a free color catalog of all our high-quality books, call toll free 1-800-542-2595 or fax 1-877-542-2596.

Library of Congress Cataloging-in-Publication Data

Names: Proudfit, Benjamin, author.
Title: Let's go to a birthday party! / Benjamin Proudfit.
Description: New York, New York : Gareth Stevens Publishing, [2020] | Series: Time to celebrate!
Identifiers: LCCN 2018044078| ISBN 9781538238820 (pbk.) | ISBN 9781538238844 (library bound) | ISBN 9781538238837 (6 pack)
Subjects: LCSH: Birthday parties–Juvenile literature.
Classification: LCC GV1472.7.B5 P76 2020 | DDC 793.2/1–dc23
LC record available at https://lccn.loc.gov/2018044078

First Edition

Published in 2020 by
Gareth Stevens Publishing
111 East 14th Street, Suite 349
New York, NY 10003

Editor: Kristen Nelson
Designer: Katelyn E. Reynolds

Photo credits: Cover, p. 1 Rawpixel.com/Shutterstock.com; pp. 5, 9, 24 (balloons), 19 Africa Studio/Shutterstock.com; p. 7 littleWhale/Shutterstock.com; pp. 11, 17, 21, 23, 24 (presents, cake) wavebreakmedia/Shutterstock.com; p. 13 Dmytro Zinkevych/Shutterstock.com; p. 15 Monkey Business Images/Shutterstock.com.

Printed in the United States of America

CPSIA compliance information: Batch #CS19GS: For further information contact Gareth Stevens, New York, New York at 1-800-542-2595.

Contents

It is Kayla's birthday.
She is having
a birthday party!

Our class got invitations.
These tell us when
the party is.

You're invited to a

BIRTHDAY party

It's Kayla's 5th Birthday

Saturday May 16th
@ 1:30 pm

RSVP by May 2nd

Kayla's house is decorated.
There are balloons.

APPY BIRTHDAY

We each wear
party hats!
They are colorful.

We eat lunch
at the party.
It is pizza!

We play games
at the party.
Frannie wins a prize!

Everyone brings Kayla presents.

What's inside?

Time for cake!
It tastes yummy!

What a fun party!
Whose birthday
is next?

Words to Know

balloons

cake

presents

Index

CELEBREMOS LAS FIESTAS ESTADOUNIDENSES / CELEBRATING U.S. HOLIDAYS

¿Por qué celebramos EL DÍA DE LOS PRESIDENTES?

Why Do We Celebrate PRESIDENTS' DAY?

Patty Swinton

Traducido por / Translated by Ana María García

PowerKiDS press

New York

Published in 2019 by The Rosen Publishing Group, Inc.
29 East 21st Street, New York, NY 10010

First Edition

Translator: Ana María García
Editorial Director, Spanish: Nathalie Beullens-Maoui
Editor, Spanish: Rossana Zúñiga
Editor, English: Brianna Battista
Book Design: Reann Nye

Photo Credits: Cover Alex Pix/Shutterstock.com; p. 5 Ariel Skelley/DigitalVision/Getty Images; p. 6 wavebreakmedia/Shutterstock.com; p. 9 Miljan Mladenovic/Shutterstock.com; p. 10 https://en.wikipedia.org/wiki/File:Gilbert_Stuart_Williamstown_Portrait_of_George_Washington.jpg; p 13 Pigprox/Shutterstock.com; p. 14 Everett Historical/Shutterstock.com; p. 17 DavidNNP/Shutterstock.com; p. 18 Shu-Hung Liu/Shutterstock.com; p. 21 Courtesy of the Library of Congress; p. 22 KidStock/Blend Images/Getty Images.

Cataloging-in-Publication Data

Names: Swinton, Patty.
Title: Why Do We Celebrate Presidents' Day? = ¿Por qué celebramos el Día de los Presidentes? / Patty Swinton.
Description: New York : PowerKids Press, 2019. | Series: Celebrating U.S. Holidays = Celebremos las fiestas estadounidenses | Includes index.
Identifiers: LCCN ISBN 9781538335215 (library bound)
Subjects: LCSH: Presidents' Day–Juvenile literature. | Presidents–United States–History–Juvenile literature.
Classification: LCC E176.8 S95 2019 | DDC 394.261–dc23

Manufactured in the United States of America

CPSIA Compliance Information: Batch #CS18PK: For Further Information contact Rosen Publishing, New York, New York at 1-800-237-9932

CONTENIDO

CONTENTS

El Día de los Presidentes
se celebra
el tercer lunes de febrero.

Presidents' Day is the third
Monday in February.

El Día de los Presidentes
es un día para aprender
sobre los presidentes
de Estados Unidos.

Presidents' Day is a day to learn
about American Presidents.

El presidente vive
y trabaja en la **Casa Blanca,**
en Washington, D. C.

The president lives and works
in the **White House**. It is in
Washington, D.C.

George Washington fue nuestro primer presidente.
Nació el 22 de febrero de 1732.

George Washington was our first president. He was born on February 22, 1732.

El **Monumento a Washington** honra al presidente George Washington. Es el edificio más alto de Washington, D. C.

The **Washington Monument** honors George Washington. It is the tallest building in Washington, D.C.

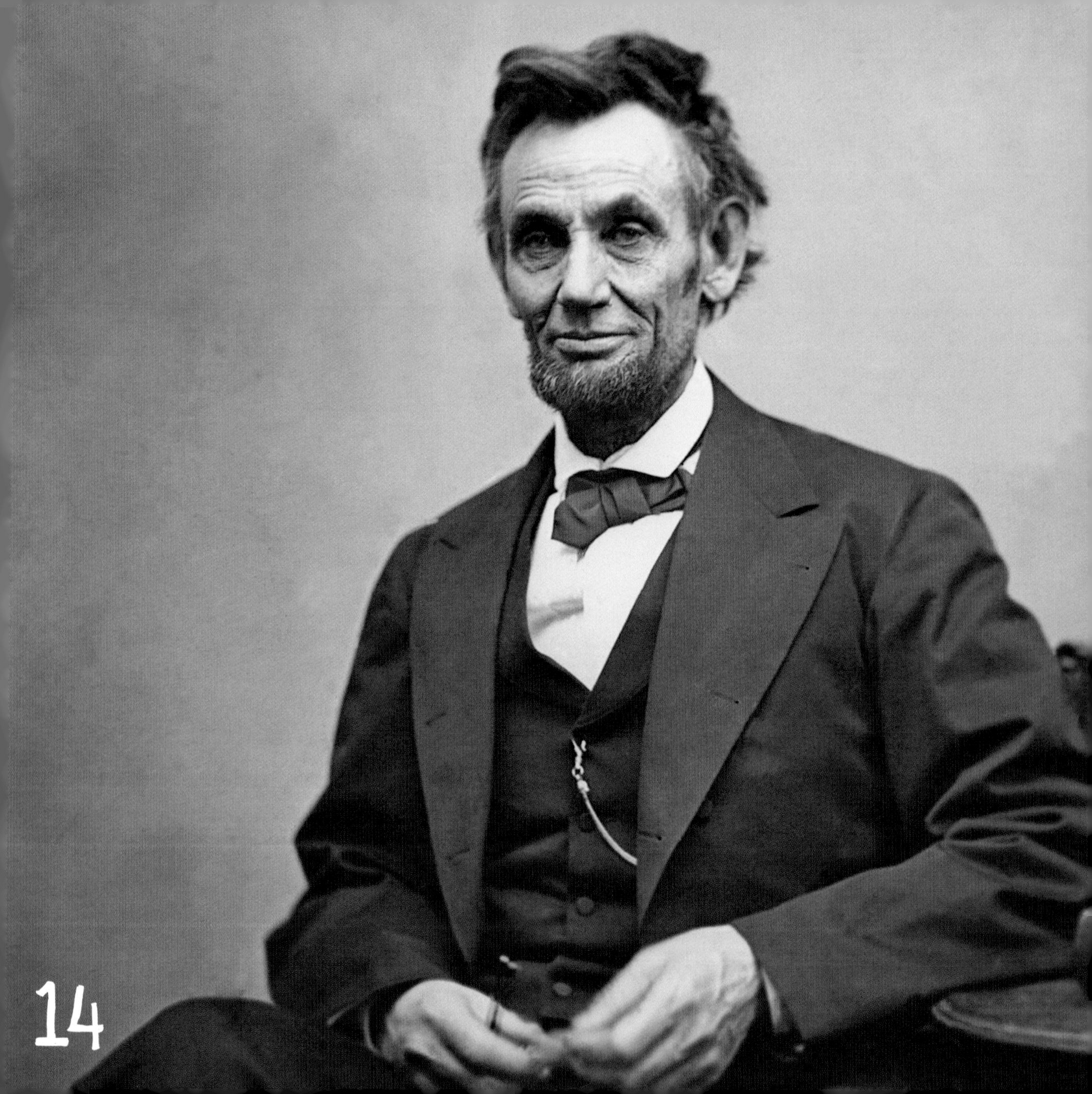

El Día de los Presidentes también reconoce a Abraham Lincoln. El presidente Lincoln nació el 12 de febrero de 1809.

Presidents' Day also honors Abraham Lincoln. Lincoln was born on February 12, 1809.

El **Monumento a Lincoln** también se encuentra en Washington, D. C. Lincoln fue el presidente más alto de Estados Unidos.

The **Lincoln Memorial** is also in Washington, D.C. Lincoln was America's tallest president.

IN THIS TEMPLE
AS IN THE HEARTS OF THE PEOPLE
FOR WHOM HE SAVED THE UNION
THE MEMORY OF ABRAHAM LINCOLN
IS ENSHRINED FOREVER

El Monte Rushmore muestra a cuatro presidentes estadounidenses. Este monumento se encuentra en Dakota del Sur.

Mount Rushmore shows four American presidents. It is in South Dakota.

Estados Unidos ha tenido
¡45 presidentes desde 1789!

America has had 45 presidents
since 1789!

AMERICAN PRESIDENTS. FIRST HUNDRED YEARS.

1776 1876

Y tú, ¿cómo celebras
el Día de los Presidentes?

How do you celebrate
Presidents' Day?

Palabras que debes aprender / Words to Know

(el) Monumento a Lincoln
Lincoln Memorial

(el) Monumento a Washington
Washington Monument

(la) Casa Blanca
White House

Índice / Index

Sitios de Internet / Websites

Debido a que los enlaces de Internet cambian constantemente, PowerKids Press ha desarrollado una lista en línea de sitios de Internet relacionados con el tema de este libro que se actualiza regularmente. Utiliza este enlace para acceder a la lista: www.powerkidslinks.com/ushol/pres

Due to the changing nature of Internet links, PowerKids Press has developed an online list of websites related to the subject of this book. This site is updated regularly. Please use this link to access the list: www.powerkidslinks.com/ushol/pres